See You Soon

Miller Williams Poetry Series
EDITED BY BILLY COLLINS

See You Soon

Poems by Laura McKee

THE UNIVERSITY OF ARKANSAS PRESS
FAYETTEVILLE

2016

for Ari

Series Editor's Preface

When the University of Arkansas Press asked if I would act as editor for the coming year's annual poetry prize named in honor of Miller Williams, the press's cofounder, long-time director, and progenitor of its poetry program, I was quick to accept. Since 1988 when he published my first full-length book, *The Apple That Astonished Paris,* I have felt indebted to Miller, who died in January 2015 at the age of eighty-four.

When he first spotted my poetry, I was forty-six years old with two chapbooks only. Not a pretty sight.

I have him to thank for first carrying me across that critical line dividing *no book* from *book*, thus turning me, at last, into a "published poet." I was especially eager to take on this task because it is a publication prize that may bring to light other first books. In fact, from the beginning of his time at the press, it was Miller's practice to publish one poet's first book every year. Then in 1990 this commitment was formalized when Miller awarded the first Arkansas Poetry Prize. Fittingly, it was renamed the Miller Williams Poetry Prize after his retirement and has grown to welcome work from both published and unpublished writers alike.

Miller Williams was more than my first editor. Over the years, he and I became friends, but even more importantly, before my involvement with the press, he served as a kind of literary father to me as his own straightforward, sometimes folksy, sometimes witty, and always trenchant poems became to me models of how poems could sound and how they could go. He was one of the poets who showed me that humor could be a legitimate mode in poetry—that a poem could be humorous without being silly or merely comical. He also showed me that a plain-spoken poem did not have to be imaginatively plain. Younger poets today could learn much from his example, as I did.

Given his extensive and distinguished career, it's surprising that Miller hasn't enjoyed a more prominent position on the American literary map. As his daughter became well known as a singer and recording artist, Miller became known to many as the father of Lucinda Williams. Miller and Lucinda even appeared on stage together several times performing a father-daughter act of song and poetry. And Miller enjoyed a bright, shining moment when Bill Clinton chose him to be the inaugural poet at his second inauguration in 1997. The poem he wrote for that day, "Of History and Hope," is a meditation on how "we have memorized America." In turning to the children of our country he broadens a nursery rhyme question by asking "How does our garden grow?" Occasional poems, especially for occasions of such importance, are notoriously difficult—some would say impossible—to write with success. But Miller rose to this lofty occasion and produced a winner. His confident reading of the poem before the nation added cultural and emotional weight to the morning's ceremony.

Apart from such public recognitions, most would agree that Miller's fuller legacy lies in his teaching and publishing career, which covered four decades. In that time, he published over a dozen books of his own poetry and literary theory. His accomplishments as a writing poet and working editor are what will speak for Miller in the years to come. The qualities of his poems make them immediately likeable and pleasurable. They sound as if they were spoken, not just written, and they show a courteous, engaging awareness of the presence of a reader. Miller knew that the idea behind a good poem is to make the reader feel something, rather than to merely display the poet's emotional state, which usually boils down to some form of misery. Miller also possessed the authority of experience to produce poems that were just plain wise.

With these attributes in mind, I began the judging of this year's prize. On the lookout for poems that Miller would approve of, that is, poems that seemed to be consciously or unconsciously in the Miller Williams School, I read and read. But in reading these scores of manuscripts, I realized that applying such narrow criteria would be selling Miller short. His tastes in poetry were clearly broader than the stylistic territory of his own verse; he published poets as different from

one another as John Ciardi and Jimmy Carter. I readjusted and began
to look for poems I thought Miller would delight in reading, instead
of echoes of his own poems. This took some second-guessing, but
I'm confident that Miller would enthusiastically approve of this year's
selections.

Broadening the field of judgment brought happy results. The
work of four very different poets, who have readability, freshness of
language, and seriousness of intent in common, stood out among the
stack of submissions.

Andrew Gent's *[explicit lyrics]* is a fascinating collection of poems
that slip through their own cracks and seem to vanish before the
reader's eyes. Influences are a matter of guesswork, but I'd say he has
learned some of his admirable tricks from Yannis Ritsos and some
of the New York School. Surprises lurk on almost every page. *See
You Soon,* the casual title of Laura McKee's book, contains poems of
powerful feeling that seem composed in the kind of tranquility of
recollection, which Wordsworth recommended. Living in a country
that appears to be continually involved in war on many fronts, readers
will find in Brock Jones's *Cenotaph* a new way of thinking and feeling
about the realities of combat. It is difficult to write war poetry because
the subject is pre-loaded with emotional weight, but Jones more than
manages to render precisely the mess of war with tenderness and
insight. Joe Wilkins's poems are located in the tradition of the sacred,
but holiness here is found in common experience. *When We Were Birds,*
as the title indicates, is full of imaginative novelty as well as reminders
that miraculous secrets are hidden in the fabric of everyday life.

In short we have here a gathering of young poets whose work,
I think, would have fully engaged and gladdened Miller Williams.
Because I have sat with him there, I can picture Miller in his study
turning the pages, maybe stopping to make a pencil note in a
margin. Miller's wider hope, of course, was that the poems published
in this series would find a broad readership, ready to be delighted and
inspired. I join my old friend and editor in that wish.

—Billy Collins

Acknowledgments

"Dream with Brancusi Nude," "Also Swans Flew Overhead," and "'It will be advantageous to realize the difficulty of the position.'" appeared in *MiPOesias*. Excerpt from "Black Green Red Yellow," "A Skeleton, A Dawn," and "'The Moment of Influence Opens, Then Ends'" were published at *Cerise Press*. "Bonneville Broad Blue," "'The pencil makes the dark.'" and "'Do you think one should always follow one's heart?'" appeared in *Poetry Northwest*. "Discover the Golden You" and "'The Order of History Is Frequently Confused'" were set as art songs by Nick Trotter, and performed by Stephanie Lavon Trotter at Gallery 1412. "Good Behavior" won the 2012 Virginia Arts of the Book poetry contest and was produced as a broadside with ink drawing for plate by Frank Riccio, and typeset by Kevin McFadden.

Many, many, many thanks to the artists and editors noted above, and equally many to my colleagues at Cornish College of the Arts. Maxine Richard, thank you for granting use of your gorgeous print for the cover. Gary Craig, thank you for all the books. Parents, sisters! Shapiro Hollanders! Erin Rants, Robin Koenig, Adrienne Bolyard, Gretchen Shantz, Carol Pecot, Suzanne Bottelli, Holly Bine, and Betsy Aoki!

Contents

See You Soon

The Order of History Is Frequently Confused

I do not love you yet;
I do not love you yet

like an extravagant property lowered from above.

Nor do I truly know you.
Do I need to? To be accurate,
maybe. To be closer,

no. This is a basic world
we are unfolding
down onto a temporary time
long before electricity comes back
on. The early spring camellia
opening I hear after.

Last One

After the battle I heaved my ax away into the swamp. For the moment it sank down through its last neck, all of its faces overcame me and I sank down too to still be here. Least one. Surrounded. Uncamouflaged. What is a swamp? Poor drainage. What is a swamp? No living. What is a swamp? Gateway to the underworld. What is a swamp? I can remember everything. Then it all comes back.

Neither a Door Nor Divide

(for H.B.)

1.
I wish to commemorate all famous acts
and begin with as usual you are standing
in your driveway, raving about your deodar
which is obviously a type of cedar I can say
with confidence once I look it up later.

2.
Sometimes you also mention the rare blue poppy
that you lifted somewhere from the earth to place
at the foot of your tree. Sincerely, their loss.

3.
Raccoon hybrid animal, half
cat-like, half bear-like, in love
with garbage, a good climb,
a good nap, a pile.

4.
This spring, Joel woke up and climbed high into the limbs
of the deodar as if he were a member of the local dance
department. Also, you report some ideas that might change
the way we think about the world and turn increasingly
away from your work on floors to the garden.

5.

The garden, the garden, not the window, earth
creeping over, the doorsill not the door, the trees,
not the house, neither a door nor divide,
the beautiful apparent deodar standing over up-
right in the moonlight in place of it. When you are not
replacing floors, you are not replacing floors.

6.

By now, many of your flowers are taller than you.

7.

You have two crows who come and go, reliably
hungry, as down-at-heel
as salesmen or an affordable destination.

8.

Sometimes you also mention the rare blue poppy,
that we can have no idea what will happen next.
Neither do we know what will be there
the moment it is needed.

9.

Under no uncertain terms are you aware the mint
on the south side of the house has gone wild
and will soon ruin the drive.
These words will have to do.

The sentinels, the scavengers, the pickers, the gliders, the hungry, the lookers.

Ephraim says beautiful is so 70s. Olivia
has a broken arm and her one good hand
caught in a raccoon trap. Bradley picks out a waltz
slowly from memory the way Andy speaks of soul searching
the way we all know our keys are somewhere
here. Robin describes the morning her neighbor's house caught
blazing fire at dawn, and everyone gathers, and everyone is safe.

Fire Department

The apartment across the alley caught fire. The firemen came
and put the fire out. The way they swarmed the building
made me feel like Dido at Carthage, overcome with rage
for one so oblivious and fortune-chosen. It was spring.
All night the engine lights discovered every detail of the coast—
the building—as they looked and bided and put out. I want to say
so what if the gods can see you. You barely know where you are
going as you creep back out to sea fixed up in my beautiful language.
Afterwards, as I wandered through the firemen cleaning up the scene
in their heavy coats and helmets, I saw her dressed as one just before
I disappeared, which split me, knowing so then how much you are loved.

A Skeleton, A Dawn

Who cares about the beginning. You can see
it's attached right here. The rising sun
 pulls its golden blind and inventories:
 back of the skull, shoulder blades, rib
 cage, pelvis. Robins, flicker. Arms
beside, legs in a line. There is a check
lately in all my answers that is incorrect,
but also legitimate, reaction to the counter-
weight of the arc. I do not like where
this is going, I say to my complete,
silent guest, suspended from the window,
nothing, nothing like us, warm in the sun.

Mint Condition

When you "entertain the thought of abandoning the path because
[your] emotional poverty is unendurable," then I am pleased
"to offer you this rare woman's cape robe. It is very beautiful,
decorated with . . . tassels . . . [and] . . . very long and narrow fictional
[stet] sleeves." Why is the medical examiner's truck parked on my
street? Do not worry, and do not worry if you do not under-
stand. Because you read all your poems at birthday parties
dressed as a clown doesn't mean you're a poet. I
have often wondered this myself from the office of does it help
and if it doesn't what does? How much of the costume must
be visible to count? In the lay of history there are hundreds
of years where nothing helps. "Where are the ladies with the
microphones?" Where are the towels? When we are lucky
architectural styles favor short distances between pillars
and/or I hear you and/or renaissance.

Sunrise Cleaners

Awareness of what one is building
being deeply flawed and that anyway
is what one is building—   The snaking double rail of shirts hangs
                               in the window like a frame of a stalled

closeness toward which the mind
falls, action   motion picture. Even though the shop
in a box that is   is closed, I can still hear the technician
                               swearing at the machine somewhere

perceivable. The city, the wilderness,
slowly changing canyon walls   in the dark. Also, the thundering
grainy hallways. Back, back   missing heartbeats in those not-chests
                               or the runner who passed me earlier—

into morning. Down again at breakfast,
serious and nervous as if to audition
                               fleet animal who has stopped abruptly,

for an example of something
one can handle. Deemed
enough, the moment is   which I understand
                               when I catch up.

a position, personnel.
Beloved extraordinary,   A river of ice ramifies the hill
choosing one must be   the whole way down, as if
                               from an aerial position.

what it seems now what
one hopes that language is—   We walk a great estuary
the device nothing is like,   slowly, one after
                                 another ghost of breath,

propensity hidden
inside all along.   the whole way down.

Seabeck Constellations

An overlap of outlines, the empty
set in motion. Branch to branch.
The king of the forest rhododendrons grooms
his wing during the neighbors' story of their friend
who threw a safe off a bridge. It wouldn't open.
Nor did the watermelon for just our eyes.
These are tools and their subjects are closed. Inside
us all this morning, the fishermen returned across
the Sound in a collapsible boat, baskets empty
except for the sea star whose eleven legs hung briefly
in the sky when it was returned. Then the boat was folded
back into a narrow spine not daylight and put
another way I saw but didn't know.

El Camino 1

Fatherless daughter of Flavia Tewksberry likes birds. She has caused large aviaries to be built on the farm in El Camino. Parakeets, canaries. The water district is bankrupt. At 2am, the birds are quiet. Flavia's daughter's grandson, my father, is lying in the middle of the living room floor because the farm's time for its district water ration is just after about now. Get up and go out. The slow dark coastal air is warm and ticking. I know you are recently made motherless and that it is difficult, but go out now and open the pipes and listen for it. It means less more even now, but it is real. The rows stretch into nothing and there is shouting to watch it carefully and the under sound of water out. Really, it is how all of us are made.

Every Problem Has a Solution

Above us, the air is occupied. A vocalist stands on the balcony
as if to coax a bird to her hand. "Once, I could not fit a piano
in my room so I left it suspended outside the window
and went downstairs." Evening. Mid-air. The black, crow-
backed shape rotates, recedes. Slowly, the black, crow-
backed shapes recede.

Also Swans Flew Overhead

For one week, everything I touched was a disaster.
The wind never stopped blowing. Listen, I said
to the surface of the lake, you're making it impossible
for me to sleep. I was hoping an accusation would help
with the isolation or serve to mitigate an earlier feeling
I had experienced in a field—two feelings, rather—
many years prior. One, that I had discounted more
than I should have; two, that a gesture of good will
was at that moment ludicrous. The ludicrous air
full of water and the quality of light a light only possible
at the ludicrous verge of a downpour where once I was made
in broken stems the color of weak gold silent as an animal.

The Petition

You have a letter from the clinic that explains your absence and that you are ill, but I understand it is also more. I have studied the careful wording of your petition and it is there in the pacing. I think there is someone you are starting to love or it is a problem you are beginning to understand is larger than you pretended and that you must make something of it. Who it is or what you do with it is none of my business. How long will these people sit around this table saying nothing in the partial sunlight. The branches of the great tree move like they are carefully searching. A small bird with a haloed eye quickly is rifling the flowers in all directions. I too have spent years consumed with jealousy. It is a completely physical experience.

Compensation

This is no way to reinvent the wheel, Richard, but if it were shaped like compensation these days you couldn't bring yourself to market without inviting months of occupational therapy or some kind of deep invasive work on your lumbar, or both. The seasons slip by like sleek private cars. I feel sure I must be missing something. Sometimes I stand by the road with a sign, but I haven't quite mastered the *je ne sais quoi* of it. My long unfocused lines are forced left on the margin at the critical moment to end vertically in a shrinking hand. What a coward. Now last week I saw a woman with the best sign and it seemed so clear: "I am very angry." It was so exactly right. She should be paid well for that.

Happiness

Outside Bonneville, the honey man sets up roadside on Sundays
with a sandwich board and a tower of jars. Oh, the honey man,
I exclaim with relief when I see him there as we are leaving
as if I knew him, or had known and forgotten. Everyone else
gathers near the dam in the early hours in hopes of catching a fish.
The poles line the shore like a flimsy barricade and the fish sail over
in the right direction or the wrong direction. It is not a case,
he would say, of one or another. I know, I say to the out-
look, as if I do, or had known and forgotten.

Good Behavior (White Salmon)

The transplant floats at the center of his eye
like a miniature of a city. Summer lightning
is and then deracinates. We can feel it
on our skin. All around us. Love
for the ground. Adherence to that love.
It makes me nervous. We walk out again
to the edge of the bluff. The power has been out
for hours. Townspeople call to one another
up and down the streets behind us casually enough
that this must happen often. What is electricity
exactly because there is strangely less resistance
without it; the winds page through. Quieter,
but also easier. Swifts take up the heated air
in long easy stitches. I lean over to start
a game of telephone. Some vacation, I say.
No kidding. So much for civilization.

"The Moment of Influence Opens, Then Ends"

During a flood, our house catches fire.
Smell of burnt sugar. The leaves are finally falling.
I say finally, I think I mean rather that last night
I dreamed we could speak truthfully to one another
at last. Your physical body was a collection
of sticks. Something to climb, except the sticks
only lead to spaces. Every time I move
to lay a hand on your shoulder, for example,
my arm just slips through. Like a difficult subject,
one stares with commitment at the words
and comprehends the words, but they do not add up.
They have come for the space. We are about to emerge
from the forest. From a nearby hill, I can see us
making our way to the edge of the distance, speaking
with animation beneath clouds shaped like anvils.
The movement catches my eye.
We make a striking pair.

Response to Fragment 17

*"Pythagoras may well have been the deepest in learning of all men.
And still he claimed to recollect details of former lives, being in one a
cucumber and one time a sardine."*

—Heraclitus / tr. Haxton

1.
Dream of the Cucumber

It's not what you think.
It's why at all, and why
so organized? Sun-
light to push the long day forward.
No one to talk to. At night
insects, stars, smell of the earth
cooling. This is no place for infinity.
I am changing my end for a way back
to the beginning. Where else
is the vine it becomes in time.

2.

Dream of the Sardine

I don't feel so alone anymore,
but I worry I have compromised
on personal destiny. Still,
those months when the shoal closes in
on the moon across the surface
take my breath away. Why
must I always be in the middle?
Who is making the decisions?
Sometimes I dream that I am alone again,
suspended in a vast blue hall,
the thrill of direction diminished.
I miss the guesswork.

Send Me Your Gold

I am writing you to say I saw the empty container
headed north again, splitting direction like a black prow the black
sea. It has been raining all afternoon. The world becomes to me
like a word painted on the side of a box is not
a message, is no reply.

September

I swam out to the rocks where the tidal purple starfish hang
on the point of the land at the edge of the world until the islands
pick up. It was strange to be out in open water this late
in the year this far north, but the other swimmer said I should try
and she was right. Few things are as hard as they seem. I stood up
slowly to look back at the shore then westward then back
and stillness ran along the shore like a missing train. While I was away
more had arrived and the narrow little cove now easily held a crowd.
Sunlight, in place of bonfires warmed the charcoal-covered sand.
Water carried their voices across. From that place
it seemed all of us were there.

Everything You Don't See Results Now

The hotel swimming pool is filled with furniture
as if someone had anticipated how one might climb
from the water or what would we hold onto
if something went wrong. The action
manifests great attention—each one balanced
against another. Not diving emptiness, but a plan
with a deep commitment to location.
Those at the base are distorted, those
at the top uncertain for any commotion. This pool
is very much like coming upon a project in the middle
of nowhere, which feels like a weakness
in the odds. I could not, however, have said this before.

Black Green Red Yellow

(for J.G.)

1. (Sweetbox)
At the start of a minor tremor, recently,
I was for a moment without means
to knowledge of it—a split second with nothing
to know. In that deeper underlying peaceful
condition, everything was also happening.
I wish I could say I memorized something accurate there.
I think about it all the time, its lack of shape or quality,
that now I must reimagine us without examples, neither at
sea nor a loss, one by one once again through the dark.

2.
To stand up from beside the river
and signs, leave one's knife
                            to the sunlight, proof
                            of having never wished for something
            to know. Only mountains,
crossing, rest,
meeting. The green dark green
country enough.
Green.

3.
The nineteenth century hand-
tinted illustration of the scarlet
coral has resisted me for months,
perfect and folded around the last place
I looked. I am not one to know everything
about the value of an edition.
I have lost my place. I do not see myself;
rather, I see myself tearing down
curtain after curtain after the site
where the town has changed.

4. (Switching Forever between Two Directions / Toledo)
We have divided everything and I will stay here.
At the top of an old fortress city, myriad
canaries change the dark to windows. Day
break. Across the bridge, blank egrets stalk the river
with more luck than travelers killing time on the banks beside make-
shift poles. This is as far as I go. On my way back, a golden light's
gold hurries after the officials who are bent in conversation over
who will improve the past. Have I mentioned my riches?
Then I cover all the cages.

Artist Island

I believe there is a small island off the coast of Mexico or Central America, perhaps two islands, interconnected by rocky outcroppings that create sheltered stretches of water in which one can swim from one part of one island to the other. The island is crowded because we all want to live there. There is a corporate presence, but it exists hostilely within a culture that is deeply suspicious of it. Every now and then executives try to flee Artist Island and they are fished from the sea, clinging to rafts of soaked currency. Musicians and rescue dogs walk the beaches for this very reason. Many years ago, they once tried to escape the island in a frenzy of development. They brought in earthmovers and dug for a week until they hit the water table. We go there every Sunday to dive, where the long armed machines were left posed at the bottom of the hole like statues of a great wreck. In the clear deep silent water, we discuss what our lives were like before Artist Island. Lines of bubbles sentence and dreams pass up our faces. Sometimes it makes me light headed. Far above us, the sun floats like a raised coin overhead. But it is not a coin. It is the sun.

Amuse-Bouche

In the afternoon we read about crocodilians, some of whom can swim twenty miles an hour in water, affecting my focus as I drive slowly down our street. I'm sorry, neighbor children, I can't help but think of your chances. A crocodilian should be your mother. In dangerous times she will hide you in her mouth to suggest she has eaten you first. She will watch over you until you are ready to leave. Then the conversation turns to our plans in the fall, which strangely involve feeding father to a fox where he will live on happily inside our new family pet. I told you you should have said yes to the dog. The six year old is obsessed with traps. It is his way to make what he wants into a trap for what prevents him from attaining it. When people ask after you we'll tell them you are right here and point to the fox.

Balzac

I like the way you handle your hang-ups.
For example, unlike you, mine make me angry.
When they are revealed and not catered to
I resort to Balzac of all people and mutter insults
based in his world. Fishwife, mostly,
because of the idea of bulging eyes and the inability
to change one's situation. You must have read
different books, I think angrily to myself
as I slap another flounder down on the ice.

The lake, the mine, the mind, the survivor, the living.

1.
It is hot in a mine the farther down
you go. That down into the earth
if the power fails, the mine floods
in the dark. Some have thought
to make it a hot house; some
have thought to mark the way
by turning on the lights.
You are a survivor and know to think,
is this a trap? We play both sides
when we talk, an underground train,
a hot air balloon, like remembering
how to make a paper box. The list says to
remember the last step is a sharp breath
into it to make the diamond form take on
all sides. I feel is this entropy or one's group
identity? I feel is this a lake with a diagram
of its topography? The fish school across

2.

on shelves one day we cross to to catch them
in the middle. The captain is sharing his lake
he knows almost completely with us,
tirelessly jumping back and forth
between the wheel and the outboard

beneath us where the forms glide
back and forth. A southwester knocks us
forward on the blank edge of the waves
above the silence the blare of the radio

in the sunlight in the middle

in the old daylight old lake half for half

a day in the sunlight in the middle.

Mothers

The technician, who I have made, has a head of snakes and a peacock gown. She often wears an intimidating mask. I was waiting for her one evening outside her cave. We were going to take a walk. She needed to get out more. Then a mother came up from behind and put her arms around me. I say a mother because I never understood my own, nor did she hers, I think. So this mother was unknown to me. With great kindness she led us both to a hill where we sat and looked out over the valley. At first, it was such a relief, but eventually it became tedious. I elbowed the technician whose eye I could not catch because of course she was wearing a mask. The snakes hissed quietly in the light breeze and the sun sank lower. I became irritated. Is she still there? I whispered loudly, but the technician wouldn't answer. So I waited with my creation into the night until I fell asleep.

Against Sunsets

"Because we are defined by space, we are not infinite." A center
hems us into the center of a pattern where a few things keep coming up:
fear of kitchen fires, the end of the world. Sometimes,
to make the point ourselves, a pan of oil is set burning in a field.
Then an otherworldly figure rushes forward in a foil suit
to douse it with water and the fireball that rises against the sunset
is an awful warning. Another example for us, we agree, drifting home
with the crowd, and so beautiful from a distance.

The Beautiful Six

(for R.R.)

I'll never tire how a badly thrown hoop fails
its line for another drunken pass at the
spiral. Or the sprinter's hunch
at the end of a race. Or a dropping sail.
Butterfly. Stray
newspaper. Butterfly—where, where—
slowly down. Join us here.
We're all down here now, after
all our large numbers,
after all.

You Be Me; I'll Be You

There are rules here; I feel there are more than rules. The suits, milling above the lake, are taking it seriously. I only found my way up this far because they'd thought to position platinum-haired girls downstairs with informational signs. One gets the feeling there'll be duels later after too much champagne, a vague sadness enhanced by someone sobbing into a flute about the loss of paradise. It is not me. I don't know when the holes in the north will reach us, but I do know they are coming out as expected as demonstrated by something a little more complex than my mastery of the line graph. Venus, traffic, earth, holdings, cash. And ourselves of course. No animals were harmed in the making of this.

The Unicorn

Disappears. Never was. Lost at the airport when I was over pleased with some nonchalant answers in customs and lost control of the luggage cart. And then the book was gone. Effingham, just rescued from a night on the bog, already screwing up enlightenment. Hannah backing back into her golden sphere. Immediately I tried to recall every detail of the pacing of the scene in the music room. The idea of another copy offends me. Ask anyone what happens after the original is gone. How has your life been? Now I'll never understand.

Think Safety First

1.
At the end of the day on the flat road at the top of experience
skeleton woman likes to put on flesh and run

voluptuous through the dusk
bones stripping off breath like the sound of a fine dress

      into shreds; into
      while the sun falls down

forward and forward, mouth open wide over the top of a puzzle:
You come to a fence. Describe the fence; how do you get past it?

Describe it correctly and those flickering permutations are footfalls
around it. The dog howl is when I am close. Describe it to me
without memory or gestures or kindness. The sun is the shadow of
an eye for getting past it. Think safety first. Not a soul for miles.
Not a stitch on either side of a violet amplitude: how do you get past it?

2.
One day I was happy: like those lesser known alchemists, ensconced
in someone's perennial indoor acreage, paid for years without result
until mid-way through dinner one evening an explosion
and a terrible smell from that occupied wing and no hope of remains
and for whom. I carry them in my mind like a bowl of leaded glass

inside of which the guests crack jokes,
inside of which weak laughter candles.

One night at night I see a cabinet of bowls—the entries
for the shape of the universe contest are full of water and quick
with over-chlorinated goldfish.

3.

One day, on her way to the ferry, skeleton woman comes across a horse
in the road. Cleverly, she tries to lure it back into its field: "Horse,

here is a puzzle: You come to a fence. Describe the fence;
how do you get past it?"

The horse dances up to her and turns into a circum-
ambulation, replying: "Death is inside of it and life is

around it." Skeleton woman leaves a note for the owner:
Your horse was in the road, please call.

4.

One day I was happy: like those hugely chattering women
articulating miniature skeletons at the back of the cafe.
I carry them in my mind like a small yellow box,

like the gods who sometimes call from a pay phone in Montana,
which I keep on my desk in a globe of artificial snow. Lumbering
equivocatory stick figures, come here:

like an answer pacing the static of a tiny blizzard world
like a tiny blizzard world arriving unblessed at the ear of a giant
who moves the chair, who opens a window.
The truth is horrible or there is plenty of room.

"Ladies Night at the Hookah Lounge"

What we need around here are more ladies.

I have no idea. I mean
I know what I'm doing. I mean
who are you?

I say what I mean
on ladies night. Therefore I do not know if I will know
to do anything with you. It is almost always impossible

to resist. Lady after lady through the door.

Thank you for inviting me.

Orange

The crows are a disruption of form. So is a crowded room
I cannot wrap my head around.
False starts. Daylight. Window flash. Orange.

What Will Change Me and When Do You Become

Some of the rules you claim for the physical world
are so beautiful. We are talking over the weather
and whether or not to head north. A north wind brings the trees
into the picture. That frantic waving in the distance. I, too, frequently
almost miss the point. Because I am unsure, I want to know more,
which is not knowledge. Times are hard. The money people come out
to buy gold at hotels near the airport. Even after I sell all my gold
I have gotten nowhere. So we drive two hours northward
to watch the eagles hunt, hop-scaling the banks and trees above
the top of the river. I want to go farther than we've seen this
before. I want to get past it. If there is no answer
here, we can start over. Hunger equals visibility.

Apples

Scientist,
detective,
we disintegrate.
But when it
is time to want
everything
back, I promise
I will work back-
ward with you.

At the Fra Angelico Exhibition, Angelico

You are ahead of me in line along with all
the old Parisians.

I like listening to them complain about the wait
in the blue light

of a late December afternoon. I like the little
adjustments they make

should the need arise to outfox the guard. When all
of us finally are wall

to wall in the tiny rooms upstairs, how much we love
you. I don't say it

well because I don't quite believe, but it is as if we
have found a way

into the sun. Surreptitiously, I look at the faces of
my group

and they are not wasting any time feeling unequal
to the task.

I think the word I'm looking for is professional—of
expectations

among peers. Then, for a moment in one of the
brightest rooms

my comprehension slipped over and a wheel of shoulders
turned me through

the heat and jostle and coolness outside again
to make my way

home in the dusk.

Dream of the Ocean Chandelier

Last night in the garden, I found a bleached
hollow kale stalk off an old, old plant
and for no reason other than it fit,
jammed it on a fence spike, which ruined
the stalk as home to hundreds of pincher
bugs, which was horrible for all of us.
This led that night to a crisis in materials,
and to the dream of the ocean chandelier.
It hung in the stairwell where I stood
disproved under a fine rain of baby
crabs and sand fleas. Who would build
such a thing. I climbed up for a closer
look at the hack job of shoreline and
flotsam run through my own impervious
timing, unmanifest, I think, never once.

Alameda Alpenglow

(for A.H.)

Some would say there is real meaning in the last thing one sees before leaving home, which for me, unfortunately, recalls only an especially low moment on an heirloom rug. Stumbling forward now, vaguely slack-jawed. The ideas, I'm sure, will come later. I just need to make room for them. For example, like all the space attending that blimp on a gentle attack vector for the city at sunset. Or who took the time to paint those mountains on the side of that trailer? God, it's beautiful, maneuvering out of the lot. Watch the mirror, Richard. I choose you.

Other Animals

Recently in a meeting, I abruptly shouted that I believe in reincarnation, which surprised me, because I only mostly think about our need to believe. And mostly, I think, we need, and that we need should be reason enough for anything. I want you to have everything you want. This, however, might be a left over impulse from my grandfather, who could never say no. What other animal is so beside itself. I wonder in fact if words aren't terrible always. Is it a crown or a thorn? No. I mean will the pain be worse in my head or my side.

Torn Branches

Broken limbs. The raw side
open. Every hallmark of a last
ditch attempt. Blue air. Attempt
coolness. Leaves. Scattered
branches littering. A failed jump. Failure
to measure. Venus like a steel pin. How exactly,
how exactly was climbing every tree going to help?
A failed jump. As if damage and hugeness had struggled
in the trees. As if hundreds of miles were nothing,
Olympics strike up. Laboratory daylight leans in
to what I imagine you look like at first
light shifts aside. Extreme and rare
circumstance retying as quickly as I could
before it turns out. It turns out
dawn is the next room here.

Cross Country

Also, the long drives across country continue to infuriate me.
What I see and don't begin to, the sky talking forever, forests
taking forever to answer. I still can't read easily. I still can't start
a conversation. In little rusted towns, dogs limp around corners and
corners eat the dogs. Heat shimmers up ending after ending until we are
over animated. In one town I met a man who knew a lot of jokes.
What do you call a fish with no eyes? What did the zero say to the
eight? Because I am a natural straight man the next thing I knew

we had an audience. Then I wondered if this was love, because he
certainly did, lighting up the last minute of a good sunset.
That was strange, I thought, later, passing eighty through the starry
dark, in that it didn't seem to ought to last. I've also been told to
take up singing. I've known only a few who have, however, without
sacrificing motion. I miss the way you used to come flying around
the corner, running flat out at the top of your voice,
"the winds don't blow, the ships don't go, harder, harder."

"Do you think one should always follow one's heart?"

I was looking for a word and I was close
the way the taxi driver was close, struggling
with an umbrella by the side of the road.
There was enough wind to turn it inside out.
There was not enough to describe it accurately
again. The gutters on our house were failing.
Water poured off the roof. Oceans rose.
Someone was playing a toy piano. The car shook
in time with the windshield wipers. Of course.
Of course. Machines solve very few problems.

Choices

In the Great Basin's Starr Valley, I became concerned that response is a condition for the perception of choice, and also whether or not specialized knowledge, as an act of good faith, might falsely occasion it. Clearly nothingness scares the crap out of me. If I had to, I'd start with something unique that attempted to describe itself completely to others. Revelations, gross assumptions, the whole nine yards. Even if it never worked, I think there'd be a general sense of well being, or at least of having loved and lost. I don't think I'd feel so mistaken. A little farther and Reno's only three hours away. Thank god it's filled with answers.

Strengths and Weaknesses

The body has no head. In some stories,
this is cause to start over. Or,
to ask why. With no head,
there would be room for more.
There is also the question
of distribution. Who deserves a head?
Do I deserve mine? What if I want yours
the way a mountain lion wants the tree
line, shirking the clear night, an animal
as cut as a diamond in its mouth.
This lends a ferrous taste to reasoning
that only the body could answer
for. It's out there somewhere ahead
of me right now—the clean break
in the new snow everything follows.

El Camino 2

Daughter of Horace Lee sorts lemons and falls in love and dies when the fourth child goes wrong. There are three children who might not remember, but the census taker wrote lemon sorter carefully under occupation as he was told. The grandmother is a farmer; her sons are truck drivers. In fact they are clever and they are also poachers. They post the oldest son nephew grandson on the road while they break the animal down. She herself has left their father, but she is nearby. Lawrence now lives with Cordelia and his father and his two sons to help with the children. Signal if you see the game warden coming. He thinks he knows we're thieves.

Yellow Racer

The opposite of self-acceptance is perfection
as organized as a snake in a knot
around a stick. Progress is impossible

to re-create. It makes me want
to take up my old place—lazy wide
sweeping looks, digitalis spiking

the ditches. In the overheated countryside
I used to start stretched out against the high-
way, eyes shut to listen for the oscillation

to and fro in love with the approach
at its beginning and later the end
I'd start over from. A snake

might embody we descend from a line
so much in and of ourselves and also not
quite of this world, tangents to a curve.

"It will be advantageous to realize the difficulty of the position."

Yesterday in the wake of a jet I saw the cloud cover divide
like drapery unveiling a great work. When you next hear news of me,
no doubt I will be doing something frivolous. An alibi.
And when it is not, nothingness. In June,
the sky holds both of these potentialities
as if it were the device used by the old photographers
to keep one's head still for the duration of the picture.
The tiger swallowtails, coincidentally, have also recently emerged.
What of me remains wide open (read unheld)
looks through the air at both and looks like equivocation.

Le Chien

Although my French is rusty, I had narrowed it down to three out-comes for the little dog whose carrier was "*complètement écrasé*" at some point during the Reykjavik Paris leg of the flight. A somber group had come to meet the passengers as we debarked. I surmised grave injury, death, or alive but missing, and was leaning toward the last given the amount of shoulder shrugging and eye contact. Also the persistence of the event itself as we rose toward baggage through Charles de Gaulle's long escalator future. Twice we crossed groups in time to catch a "*oui, le chien*" or "*si, le chien*," and once a uniformed man pulling a small case with the wry smile of having lost a call, and everyone made way for him. In the austere terminal we chose our bags; I slowly bargained with a driver for an okay fare into the city. Then we were speeding toward the center, yawning, blinking at the daylight and loss of the hours. We could not decide what to do first. I have no idea what happened to the dog.

Never Displayed or Used

At the flower show, in the flooded parking lot between converted horse
trailers, we second guessed our timing. In the discount ticket line.
In the hall itself. Candid warehouse lights deepened the fake lily ponds.
The orchid specialists, surprisingly, were the most forthcoming.
They never stopped talking, sweeping back table drapery for species
waiting in the dark, or pulling examples of Saint Swithin down
from overhead to explain how the lines got crossed.
I never found the geranium master although I went back
several times—only little notes in different hands promising to be back
in five minutes or shortly or soon. Vegetable and dahlia experts loitered
in the aisles, hundreds of acres elsewhere in their minds. I wondered
what was happening with all the bodies at the tattoo convention
(that we chose between), but could only imagine and headed back
to the geranium display and thought about getting into irises because
everyone was there and looked like they were having a good time.
Follow the crowd, I thought, assemble, assemble. Then
I found the outdoor bedroom where, I admit, I lost most of my interest
in anything else. There was no getting over that much moss
in one place was incredible—a summary of everything that got me
into languages in the first place. Once for us. A perfect word.

A Level Playing Field on a Flood Plain

Traveling north and returning south is the most unbearable.
The community kitchens are hung with reminders
how much sound carries. Also, because of the budget cuts,
the lines are unreal. In the morning,
when the great talking flocks pass invisibly
off shore, I can feel the edges of my position
erode. Beauty juxtaposed with loss has driven so many
right out of their minds. Eyeshine in the firelight,
no real strategy. Now is the time it should come
to me. All these intentions. Paper curls off the trees.

Cones

We took a walk at the golden hour just before sunset
when the man in the picture leans through the atmosphere
in anticipation of the stars during which I recounted a sad story
about a time near a place I once lived, near a pine tree
at the edge of a gully. The boy's husky howled for days.
Why, this is a sad story, you said. We had stopped
beneath the pine tree because of a snapping incorrect sound
as though someone was walking slowly up through the branches
or the tree was on fire and we realized the sound was the cones
splitting open in the sunlight, and while the air filled around it,
the tree stood motionless, invisibly terrible, the way a rumor
of a local miracle or tragedy can be. Split after split directly
before me. I never heard what became of his family, I said,
as we walked back through the neighborhood; children
stole through the yards on our heels under cover
of an elaborate game at whose end later we'd compare
all the notes and see if we couldn't fill in the blanks.

Stable of Dark Horses

Outcomes. The oval of last night's rain
     hangs a deep breath
in the air—who, with a taste
   for collisions and unsorted
stalls, who prises.

I do, however, miss our walks.

The long walks around the middle tier of the hill. The work late at night
now is constant. Only five more years before the tunnel is complete. The
project seems somehow just a little too extravagant for what it achieves.
But the trucks in the moonlight are convincing, and the workers,
measuring and noting and striding the cranes, seem focused enough. I
also want to start something—a real endeavor. Something a little more
substantial than I've done before, but I am having doubts about my
training. More specifically, did I absorb anything, or does it just slip by?
Have I made the mistake of likeness? Am I only that?

Exotic Treats

Especially on long drives through the country,
you like to tell that story about your old girlfriend
whose parrot was killed one afternoon
by a raccoon who stole in through the pet door.
It was horrible, you say. Feathers everywhere.
Are you laughing? Stop laughing.
She really loved that bird.

Dream with Brancusi Nude

All week I had struggled to maintain a professional demeanor
and then a coworker implied that I didn't know what I was doing.
I didn't know what I was doing, but in the dream
I felt suddenly that I was riding an immense wave
and after calmly deflecting his comment
I called him a terrible, terrible name.
Neither of us knew what should happen next.
We began to laugh. Then, at the moment he turned away,
he slipped and fell naked upon the floor
into a breathtaking collection of planar surfaces,
becoming so still and inscrutable that I could not even recall his name.
So beautiful and cool. I knelt down to lay a hand on his chest.
This dream came to me from far below the surface of the earth.

"The pencil makes the dark."

(for N.H.)

Pine needles, tiny pivots under-
foot along the path. I see hatch marks. I
see no way until Princess You Know comes
out from behind a conglomeration
of clouds. Ta da. Oh Natural Beauty how
did you get your start? Oh Native Skill how
did you learn that? These days one needs a
fox. One great hunter to another, let us remember where
we get our chops. In the courtyard in that old valley, we'd play
hangman for hours. Then we'd dance. And that's the only reason
I'm still here because honestly I can't see and the fog hasn't even
yet rolled in, cool flank, that lucky, lucky caress.

Ballroom

Soap in hell laughter also   Oh god not candles   "the company" or
"coeur"   Richard is it   a number of others   You I
    shouldn't have given that project away   Unending jokes
out of   Save me   the coastline runs north   At least
it looks so   on the balcony   Lydia is it   one room over
    someone sneezing delicately   complexity   golden
opportunity whatever   Who does that or   who pays for that
completely out of my depth   of my choices   that lost easy
swim   no light   that lost easy   Arborist   what's your opinion
deodar   wrists out   swinging   why can't I   why
don't we   Can't remember   what doesn't last in hell   Oh hell
    not soap a snowball   So the soap would last longer right?
Step step   sorry   You is it   Vaguely flustered
are these lilies just for the summer   anyway   but you need   don't
you I don't   I need   Everyone to one side   none of
this fending   off sneezing up into the light   Who are these
people   where is my   ideal I'll trade you   this is not what
would you do   I want to do   that too

Bonneville Broad Blue

You were throwing ice to silence the frogs. Artificial
light caught the trees mid-posture under the pouring rain.
The chorus twirled forward as deafening as before.
I kept thinking about the lack of evidence if it worked
and the animated patron I had seen at breakfast,
addressing her constituency like an articulation
of the truth itself. I have a cousin just like that—
whose silvery swing swings around and around. And you,
I could listen to you for hours.

See You Soon

In the artist section I found a horrible painting of a pair of
empty pants, running along the shore in the style of Munch's
Scream (except of course there was no face). I could see, regardless,
that the artist truly wanted a resemblance. I asked my companion
what she thought and she said, it makes me wish I had worn a belt.
Then we came to a photograph of a famous place. I know that tree,
I know that tree, she exclaimed in a way that was familiar to me too,
although I had never so quickly stepped from my clothes as I did
then, leading us to decide right there this was the perfect spot
to stop and have our picnic.

"I don't believe in talent."

At Lucky Leap, I try out a new idea that goes over better: "freedom
is the opposite of cause." Recently, on the backstage tour

of the zoo kitchens, girls are hard at work over cutting boards.
Ziplocks of frozen chicks and rabbits are not for Easter.

I ride the escalator up into the city over and over. I might have
a complex, I worry, or, with a coat of shade and sunlight,

I could avoid all of this. What do you think, I ask two peacocks
who have positioned themselves improbably high

in the branches of an old tree. Here, they say, is where
our attention wanders. No one chooses to stay the course,

therefore no one stays it. A wide blue sea,
crosser, while you know how.

Discover the Golden You

At sunset. Not a hint of warmth, not a hinge
the size of a small purse though sometimes
I feel that we are cradled and put away.

We are a transitory idea.
There is great melancholy
in our language as it describes our history.

Direct experience across a distance,
surface of the lake at this time last year.
Generally what occurs is what I believe in.
Our symbolic systems

tell me what happened.
Tell me what will happen

and do not hesitate.
There is no hesitation

against the earth
as a lake as a diver above the lake
as a blank slump downward.

We are a transitory idea and there is great melancholy
in the history we keep. A quick succession
between you and the sky. If I could think of us alone.

There is a great experiment.

Notes

The titles, "'It will be advantageous to realize the difficulty of the position.'" and "'The Moment of Influence Opens, Then Ends'" are taken from the *I Ching*, translated by James Legge. "Mint Condition" contains excerpts from both the *I Ching* and the text of online auctions.

Both "Against Sunsets" and "'I don't believe in talent.'" emerged from readings in the Second Division of *Kant's Critique of Pure Reason*, translated by J. M. D. Meiklejohn. The quotations in the body of the poems are from the speaking voice in the poem, who is posing questions.